EDGE OF EXTINCTION

GORILLAS

PowerKiDS press

TRICIA HOFFMAN

Published in 2027 by The Rosen Publishing Group, Inc.
2544 Clinton Street, Buffalo, NY 14224

First Edition

Portions of this work were originally authored by Michael Portman and published as *Animals At Risk: Gorillas in Danger*. All new material in this edition is authored by Tricia Hoffman.

Editor: Tricia Hoffman
Book Design: Beeline Media and Design

Photo Credits: Cover, pp. 1 Joyce Nelson/Shutterstock.com; p. 5 Nick Biemans/Shutterstock.com; p. 6 SamSamFM/Shutterstock.com; p. 7 Martin Pelanek/Shutterstock.com; p. 8 PARALAXIS/Shutterstock.com; p. 9 Wirestock Creators/Shutterstock.com; p. 9 Dancing_Man/Shutterstock.com; p. 11 Ondrej Prosicky/Shutterstock.com; P. 13 Eric Isselee/Shutterstock.com; p. 15 Edwin Butter/Shutterstock.com; p. 17 Randy van Domselaar/Shutterstock.com; p. 18 Svetlana Foote/Shutterstock.com; p. 19 Martens Coyotes/Shutterstock.com; p. 21 (WWF) Piotr Swat/Shutterstock.com; p. 21 (devices) ArieStudio/Shutterstock.com; p. 21 (gorillas) Moneynetar/Shutterstock.com; p. 21 (tree) Photoongraphy/Shutterstock.com

Cataloging-in-Publication Data
Names: Hoffman, Tricia.
Title: Gorillas / Tricia Hoffman.
Description: Buffalo, New York : PowerKids Press, 2027. | Series: Edge of extinction | Includes glossary and index.
Identifiers: ISBN 9781499457803 (pbk.) | ISBN 9781499457810 (library bound) | ISBN 9781499457827 (ebook)
Subjects: LCSH: Gorilla--Juvenile literature. | Gorilla--Conservation--Juvenile literature. | Endangered species--Juvenile literature.
Classification: LCC QL737.P96 H644 2027 | DDC 599.884--dc23

Printed in China

CPSIA Compliance Information: Batch #QSPK27. For Further Information contact Rosen Publishing at 1-800-237-9932.

Contents

Words in the glossary appear in **bold** type the first time they are used in the text.

Gorillas in Africa

Gorillas live in the forests of central Africa. They are the largest **primates** in the world.

There are two **species** of gorillas: eastern gorillas and western gorillas. Each species can be broken into two smaller groups, or subspecies. Eastern lowland gorillas and mountain gorillas belong to the eastern species. Western lowland gorillas and Cross River gorillas are subspecies of western gorillas.

Gorillas are usually peaceful animals and have few enemies in nature. However, they still face dangers from the loss of their homes, hunters, and illness.

ON THE EDGE

A gorilla's arms are longer than its legs. Its stomach is bigger than its chest.

Gorillas can stand as tall as a human!

The Largest Gorillas

Eastern lowland gorillas live only in the forests of the eastern Democratic Republic of Congo. Eastern lowland gorillas are also known as Grauer's gorillas. They are the largest of the four subspecies. Adult males, called silverbacks, can weigh more than 500 pounds (227 kg)!

Like all gorillas, eastern lowland gorillas travel in groups to search for food. They eat many kinds of fruits and plants, including leaves, stems, seeds, and tree bark. Despite their size, these large primates are mostly **herbivores**, but will sometimes eat ants and other insects.

ON THE EDGE

Adult male gorillas have silver fur on their backs. That's why they're called "silverbacks."

A group of gorillas living together is called a troop. Eastern lowland gorilla troops may have as few as five or as many as 30 gorillas.

Eastern Lowland Gorillas in Danger

Eastern lowland gorillas face many **threats** in the wild, including **habitat** loss and **poaching**. Large parts of their forest homes have been cleared for firewood and farming. This makes it harder for the gorillas to find food. In addition, there's **mining** in the area. The miners hunt the gorillas for meat.

The number of eastern lowland gorillas has been falling fast. In the 1990s, there were about 17,000 in the wild. Today, there may be fewer than 6,000. These animals are considered critically **endangered**.

The long period of war in the Democratic Republic of Congo has made it hard for people to keep eastern lowland gorillas safe.

In the Mountains

Like the eastern lowland gorilla, the mountain gorilla is a subspecies of the eastern gorilla. Mountain gorillas live in the mountains of Rwanda, Uganda, and the Democratic Republic of Congo.

Mountain gorillas have very thick, long, black hair. It keeps them warm in the cold, misty air of the mountain forests. Though smaller than the eastern lowland gorillas, these primates are still pretty large. Males can weigh up to 400 pounds (180 kg). Females weigh about half as much. Most mountain gorillas live in groups of about 10, with one male and several females.

ON THE EDGE

Both males and females help take care of baby gorillas, which are called infants.

Mountain gorillas spend much of their day eating. At night, groups sleep together in nests on the ground or in trees.

Mountain Gorillas in Danger

The biggest threat to mountain gorillas in the wild is habitat loss. Mountain gorillas share their mountains with Africans trying to escape war. These people are changing the forests by cutting down trees. Some also set traps to catch animals such as antelope for food. Sometimes mountain gorillas get caught instead.

Being around people can be dangerous to mountain gorillas, even if those people aren't trying to do harm. People can spread illness. Even illnesses that aren't deadly to people can kill gorillas. That's because gorillas haven't built up the same immunities that people have.

ON THE EDGE

Virunga National Park was Africa's first park. The land was set aside in 1925 to protect mountain gorillas.

Today, there are about 1,000 mountain gorillas left in the wild.

Gorillas in the West

There are two subspecies of western gorillas, and both are smaller than eastern gorillas. Brown or gray hair covers their bodies. They often have reddish hair on their heads.

The western lowland gorilla has the highest population of all gorillas. There are about 320,000 western lowland gorillas in central and west Africa.

Cross River gorillas live in Nigeria and Cameroon. They live in thick forests. Scientists have found it hard to study these gorillas or even take photos of them. There may be fewer than 350 in all. They are the most endangered great ape in Africa.

ON THE EDGE

Cross River gorillas were thought to be **extinct** until some were discovered in the 1980s.

Unlike other primates, gorillas spend most of their time on the ground. They sometimes climb trees to look for food and to rest.

Western Gorillas in Danger

There are far more western gorillas in the wild than eastern gorillas. That's likely because western gorillas live in areas with far fewer humans.

Even so, poaching is a serious danger. Also, businesses are cutting down trees to sell the wood. As more of the forest is cut down, it becomes easier for poachers to find the gorillas.

Illness is also a serious threat to western gorillas. **Ebola** is one of the deadliest sicknesses in the world. It can kill all kinds of primates, including people. Some scientists think ebola killed 33 percent of western lowland gorillas in the early 2000s.

Gorillas are intelligent. They have been known to use tools to find food or solve problems.

Gorilla Babies

Female gorillas are eight to 10 years old before they can have babies. They usually give birth to one baby every four years. That means that each female will only have a few babies in her lifetime. Also, about 40 percent of gorilla babies die before they're one year old. This makes it very hard for the population to grow.

All four subspecies of gorillas are endangered. They are in danger of becoming extinct.

ON THE EDGE

Gorillas can live to be 40 years old in the wild and more than 50 years old in zoos.

For the first six months of its life, a baby gorilla is in constant contact with its mother.

Save the Gorillas!

Now, many people know about the dangers gorillas face and are working to help them. Wildlife **conservation** groups work with governments to protect gorillas and their habitats. They help create laws to stop forests from being cut down. They support groups who search the forests for poachers. They help people find food other than gorilla meat. Most importantly, they teach people about gorillas and why it's important to save them.

In recent years, gorilla populations have grown. It's a long and hard effort, but it's not too late to save these amazing animals. Everyone can work together to make a difference—and that means you can help too!

What Can You Do to Help?

Recycle old electronic devices. Many cell phones contain a mineral called coltan. Coltan mainly comes from the ground where gorillas live. Recycling means that the coltan can be reused.

Read labels. Gorilla habitats are being destroyed to plant more oil palm trees. Choose products with the Roundtable for Sustainable Palm Oil (RSPO) label on them.

Teach others. Tell friends and family members what you've learned about gorillas and how they can help save them too.

Adopt a gorilla through the World Wildlife Fund. Donate money that will go toward protecting gorilla habitats, working with local communities, and other conservation work.

Glossary

conservation: the protection of the natural world

Ebola: a disease that causes high fever, headache, muscle aches, and bleeding, and often results in death

endangered: in danger of dying out

extinct: having no living members

habitat: an area where plants, animals, or other living things live

herbivores: animals that eat only plants

mining: having to do with digging something out of the ground

poaching: illegal hunting

primate: a member of the group of animals that includes people, monkeys, gorillas, and chimpanzees

species: a group of animals that are all of the same kind

threat: something likely to cause harm

Fact Check

1. All gorillas live in ________.
   a. Asia b. Africa c. Australia

2. What is the largest subspecies of gorilla?
   a. eastern lowland gorillas
   b. mountain gorillas
   c. western lowland gorillas

3. A group of gorillas is called a ____________.
   a. school b. gaggle c. troop

Answers: 1. b, 2. a, 3. c

On the Internet

Gorillas
https://wwf.panda.org/discover/knowledge_hub/endangered_species/great_apes/gorillas/
Read about gorillas and learn how you can help them.

Gorilla
https://animals.sandiegozoo.org/animals/gorilla
Read fun facts about gorillas and see photos of them in action.

Index